FARMINGTON COMMUNITY LIBRARY

3 0036 01271 4109

THE FARMINGTON COMMUNITY LIBRARY
FARMINGTON HILLS BRANCH
32737 WEST TWELVE MILE ROAD
FARMINGTON HILLS, MI 48334-3302
(248) 553-0300

D1609679

SEP 05 2017

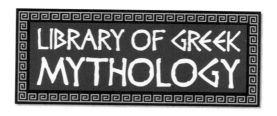

3 0036 01271 4109

Creation Stories in Greek Mythology

Titles in the *Library of Greek Mythology* series include:

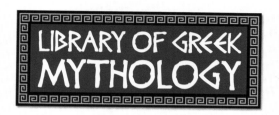

Creation Stories in Greek Mythology

Don Nardo

ReferencePoint
Press®

San Diego, CA

© 2017 ReferencePoint Press, Inc.
Printed in the United States

For more information, contact:
ReferencePoint Press, Inc.
PO Box 27779
San Diego, CA 92198
www.ReferencePointPress.com

ALL RIGHTS RESERVED.
No part of this work covered by the copyright hereon may be reproduced or used in any form or by any means—graphic, electronic, or mechanical, including photocopying, recording, taping, web distribution, or information storage retrieval systems—without the written permission of the publisher.

LIBRARY OF CONGRESS CATALOGING-IN-PUBLICATION DATA

Names: Nardo, Don, 1947-
Title: Creation stories in Greek mythology / by Don Nardo.
Description: San Diego : ReferencePoint Press, 2016. | Series: Library of Greek mythology series | Includes bibliographical references and index. | Description based on print version record and CIP data provided by publisher; resource not viewed.
Identifiers: LCCN 2015037260 (print) | LCCN 2015036588 (ebook) | ISBN 9781601529596 (epub) | ISBN 9781601529589 (hardback)
Subjects: LCSH: Cosmogony, Greek. | Creation--Mythology--Greece. | Mythology, Greek.
Classification: LCC BL795.C68 (print) | LCC BL795.C68 N37 2016 (ebook) | DDC 292.2/4--dc23
LC record available at http://lccn.loc.gov/2015037260

Contents

Ancient Greece (Circa 500 BCE)

Introduction

Origins of the Creation Tales

They looked human, each with a hair-covered head atop a muscular torso, with two equally muscular arms and two powerful legs below. But they were *not* human, for people did not yet exist. These warriors, towering to the height of the tallest trees, were immortal beings—the first race of gods to command the earth and natural elements. They called themselves the Titans.

On this day they had gathered to do battle with a group of upstarts among their own ranks. Surely, went the common assumption, these impudent rebels would easily be brought low and taught an awful lesson in humility and obedience. But this prediction of effortless victory was rudely interrupted by a sudden blast of blinding brilliance. What had been an empty patch of nearby sky was now alive with gigantic flashes of lightning. The immense bolts of pure energy leapt high into the heavens and then, while giving forth deafening claps of thunder, they shot downward on the startled Titans.

Some of those lumbering giants recoiled as the streaks of lightning fried their flesh. Others managed to dodge the bolts, but their battle ranks became confused and disrupted. Who had unleashed this astonishingly effective attack, they wondered? But before they could offer answers to this disturbing question, enormous sheets of flame, accompanied by a deafening roar, descended from high above. The nearby forests caught fire, and as they blazed, all around them the streams and lakes and even the vast oceans began to boil.

Amidst this unnatural assault, for the first time in their living memory the Titans were riddled by the primal feeling of fear. They had always believed they were the strongest force in the universe. Yet it now dawned on them that someone or something even more potent than they might exist. As they mused on that scary thought, one of their number spied sudden movement atop a nearby mountain. From its summit a monstrous blast of black smoke erupted in a volcanic torrent that rushed outward, darkening the skies all around.

Then, from within those dark, churning clouds emerged a muscular arm, with its hand grasping a dazzling thunderbolt. As the troubled Titans looked on in awe, they saw the body and face to whom that arm belonged materialize in a burst of sparkling radiance. Before them now stood their mortal enemy, who had sworn to defeat and dethrone them as nature's master race. His name was Zeus.

When the Cosmos Emerged

Thus begins the famous ancient Greek myth about the fantastically violent war between the first race of gods—the Titans—and the second divine band—the Olympians. Every boy and girl growing up in classical Greece came to learn this and several other creation stories almost from the moment they could talk. *Classical Greece* is a term that was coined by modern historians. In a general sense, it denotes the residents of Greece during the period lasting from the seventh through the fourth centuries BCE. This was the era when the Greek world was dominated by city-states, tiny nations each consisting of a central town surrounded by supporting villages and farms.

It was during that same age that a few of those states, most notably Athens, produced a spectacular burst of great art, culture, and democratic ideals. Among the ranks of the classical Greeks were the renowned philosophers Aristotle and Plato; the incomparable playwrights Aeschylus and Sophocles; the master sculptor Phidias, who decorated the Parthenon temple, now seen as the most perfect

---

WORD ORIGINS

COSMOS

In ancient Greece: the universe, or everything that exists.

In modern life: cosmology, the study of the universe's origins.

In the violent war between the immortal Titans and Olympians, the Olympian Zeus crushes his giant foes by throwing lightning bolts to start an avalanche of boulders. This story depicts the origins of the deities worshipped by the ancient Greeks.

building ever erected; and the democratic reformer Pericles, who oversaw Athens's so-called golden age of culture and art.

These individuals and their contemporaries cherished a large, rich body of creation stories and other myths. Those creation tales told how the universe, or *cosmos*, as the Greeks called it, came to be. They also

9

explained how the Titans, Olympians, and other gods, along with human beings, originated. Among the classical Greeks, the general view was that these events and characters involved in the world's formation had occurred long before their civilization existed.

The Greeks called that dimly remembered era the Age of Heroes. They viewed it as a special time in which first, the cosmos emerged from swirling masses of darkness and chaos. Then, the creation tales said, the earliest divine forces and gods appeared. The different races of gods fought among themselves for mastery of the cosmos, after which the winners decided to create humans. According to the Greek myths, those earliest people were at first weak, meek, and fearful. But they soon produced some noble, daring warriors. Those great heroes, who were said to have slain many of the menacing monsters that then walked the earth, frequently interacted with the gods.

Questioning the Muses

To the classical Greeks, their creation stories and other myths were not simply quaint tales trotted out now and then to entertain children. Rather, they looked at these stories partly as historical tracts that informed them how their world came to be. Just as people today want to know where they came from, the Greeks desperately desired to understand their own origins.

As the early seventh-century-BCE Greek epic poet Hesiod begged of some female deities called the Muses, "Tell me how the gods and earth arose at first, and the rivers and the boundless swollen sea and shining stars, and the broad heaven above." Hesiod asked the Muses to reveal "from the beginning, which first came to be?"[1] Was it the dark, swirling masses of chaos? Or was there a living being, some sort of god, alive and stirring within those jumbled, muddled masses?

The answers the Muses supposedly gave Hesiod became the basis for the classical Greeks' creation stories and other myths. They believed that the splendid, awe-inspiring period in which nature emerged and the gods created and walked among humans had long ago disappeared. Eventually, the story went, an inferior age, peopled by more ordinary men and women, emerged—namely their own era, today known as that of classical Greece.

An Eternal Tradition?

Modern historians and other scholars fortunately know considerably more about Greek history than the classical Greeks themselves did. It is now clear that the so-called Age of Heroes was in large degree a mangled memory of a real society. Close to one thousand years before Pericles, Plato, and Sophocles made history in classical Athens, mainland Greece and its nearby islands had been home to two earlier advanced peoples. Centered in the islands were the Minoans, and dwelling on the mainland were the Mycenaeans. (Both of those names were coined by modern historians; no one knows what those peoples called themselves.)

The Minoans and Mycenaeans employed tools and weapons made mainly of bronze, an alloy of copper and tin. So modern experts call that bygone era, corresponding to the Age of Heroes, Greece's late Bronze Age (circa 1600–1100 BCE). During those times, the Minoans and Mycenaeans erected strong centralized kingdoms containing powerful palace-fortresses. Those realms interacted not only with one another but also with non-Greek peoples and cities, including the ancient Egyptians and the famous trading city of Troy (in what is now Turkey). Eventually, during the period between 1200 and 1100 BCE, that entire early Greek civilization collapsed, for reasons that are still unclear and debated by scholars.

WORD ORIGINS

Muses

In ancient Greece: nine minor goddesses who oversaw literature, the arts, and science.

In modern life: muse, meaning a person who inspires someone else to be creative.

The Greek world then sank into a cultural dark age. The palace-fortresses were abandoned and fell into disrepair, while literacy, record keeping, and artistic skills were lost. Within only a few generations, Greece's once splendid Bronze Age society passed into legend. Increasingly distorted and exaggerated memories of the old kingdoms and their leading statesmen and warriors steadily morphed into myths.

Of these stories, the ones telling how the world, gods, and humans were created may have been partly based on the creation tales of the Bronze Age peoples themselves. Indeed, modern experts have shown that certain classical Greek religious beliefs and traditions were more highly developed versions of those prevalent in Bronze Age Greece. For instance, evidence shows that Zeus and some other gods prominent in the classical creation myths were directly based on deities worshipped by the mainland Mycenaeans.

Other aspects of the creation stories may have been invented by the myth-tellers themselves. Each new generation had its storytellers, called bards, some of whom traveled from village to village. They retold the old tales but sometimes embellished them by adding new plot twists and characters. Hesiod, one of the first great bards of classical Greece, is believed to have followed such literary practices himself.

Thus, the Greeks who established the world's first democracies and built the magnificent Parthenon inherited a series of creation myths from their immediate ancestors. What Aristotle, Pericles, and their colleagues did not understand was where and when those stories had originated. They did not realize that their own society was only a link in an ongoing chain of telling and retelling those tales. Today's versions, presented in movies and electronic media as well as verbally and in books, form the latest link in what may well prove to be an eternal tradition.

Chapter One

The Cosmos and Earth Emerge

Perhaps the most basic and mystifying of all the myths of the ancient Greeks were those dealing with how the world, gods, and humans came to be. Moreover, nearly all members of ancient Greek society—from farmers, to politicians, to philosophers—were fascinated by their own origins. At the time, no organized science of archaeology existed to help explore and learn about past ages. So people looked to myths to help them unravel what modern myth-teller Rhoda A. Hendricks terms "the mysteries related to the beginnings of things, and especially to the origin of the universe."[2]

In continually retelling their creation myths, in a very real sense the Greeks felt they were passing historical truths on from one generation to the next. The late noted historian Michael Grant pointed out that it was not history in the sense that people view it today. Modern history books are expected to document their contents using literary, archaeological, and other kinds of evidence.

In contrast, the ancient Greek creation myths presented what Grant called para-history, or "sort of history." Although it lacked fully documented facts, it did possess "truth of another kind,"[3] he wrote, more of an emotionally satisfying sort of reality. A person could not prove it happened but had a feeling in his or her gut and heart that it was right.

It is also significant that, as the primary founders of Western (European-based) civilization, the Greeks passed on their creation myths to later generations. Long after the ancient world faded from view, these tales were perpetuated as part of the very fabric of Western society. The "effects of this mythical para-history of ancient times," Grant continued, "can easily be traced onwards from then to now. It can be traced in the conscious and unconscious reliance of every intervening generation—of whatever era—upon the ways of thinking and ideas manifested by these mythologies." Furthermore, he adds, "as a readily apparent proof of its durability, the writers of the twentieth century showed themselves every bit as conscious of their mythical inheritance as any of their predecessors."[4] In other words, modern observers were no less fascinated by the Greek myths than the ancient Greeks themselves had been.

The "Beginnings of All Things"

No matter which century the inheritors of the Greek creation stories lived in, they immediately recognized one unique and vital aspect of these tales. Namely, they exhibit a point of view of world and human origins that is quite different from those of most later peoples. The ancient Christians, for example, along with their modern descendants, believed that a divine being—usually called simply God—created the cosmos. But the Greeks held a polar-opposite view. The great modern myth-teller Edith Hamilton noted that they "did not believe that the gods created the universe. It was the other way about. The universe created the gods."[5] This singular, important aspect of the classical Greeks' religious thinking sprang directly from descriptions of the creation in their myths.

A number of surviving ancient literary works, including poems, plays, and philosophical tracts, contain accounts of or mention the Greek version of the creation of the cosmos, heaven, and earth. Among these writings, by far the most detailed and important is an epic poem, the *Theogony*. That word translates into English roughly as "lineage of the gods." The author was Hesiod, a well-to-do Greek farmer from the region of Thebes, in the central Greek mainland, who flourished in the early 600s BCE.

Before there were any gods at all, Hesiod begins, all that existed was an immense, ill-defined collection of unknown substances known as Chaos. Floating within this primeval assortment of materials, as one modern expert puts it, were "the seeds or beginnings of all things."

Before the birth of the gods, the Greeks believed, all that existed was Chaos (as depicted in this eighteenth-century engraving). The earth, sky, air, and light grew from this dark and disorganized state of being.

They "were mixed up together in a shapeless mass, all moving about in all directions."[6]

During the long ages that Chaos existed in the same disorganized state, its surface remained pitch black thanks to two dark, prehistoric forces called Night and Erebus. According to the fifth-century-BCE playwright Aristophanes, "No spark of light was visible within that seemingly unending dark realm. There was no earth yet, nor air, nor sky." Then, without warning, Night and Erebus became living,

Myth-Tellers' Corner: Hesiod

Along with the famous Homer, Hesiod was one of the two first major writers, as well as epic poets, revered by the classical Greeks. No one kept historical records in Hesiod's day. So it is impossible to tell exactly when he was born. It was likely sometime in the late 700s BCE, and he seems to have done most of his writing in the early 600s BCE. Like his brother, Perses, he was a farmer in Boeotia, the region of central Greece dominated by Thebes. Hesiod also advised some of his neighbors on legal matters. These and a few other facts about Hesiod are known because he mentioned them in passing in his short epic poems, *Works and Days* and the *Theogony*. The latter deals mainly with the early Greek myths of creation, including how the cosmos and earth formed from Chaos, as well as the rise of the Titans, the earliest race of gods. In the opening section, Hesiod claims that the Muses, nine divine daughters of the god Zeus, had inspired him to tell the story of the creation. "Hail, daughters of Zeus!" the passage begins. "Give me sweet song, to celebrate the holy race of gods who live forever. Tell how the gods and earth arose at first, and rivers and the boundless swollen sea and shining stars, and the broad heaven above, and how the gods divided up their wealth and how they shared their honors, how they first captured Olympus with its many folds. Tell me these things, Olympian Muses."

Hesiod, *Theogony*, in *Hesiod and Theognis,* trans. Dorothea Wender. New York: Penguin, 1982, p. 26.

conscious beings. Though almost formless and extremely primitive and crude, they did possess the power of reproduction, and "from within the spinning winds inside Erebus's breast appeared an egg."[7]

At first, that large, ill-defined seed was as dark as the rest of Chaos. But that soon changed. The egg suddenly cracked open, and out popped Eros, the essence of purest love, who had, Aristophanes continued, "shining gold wings sprouting from his shoulders." With those wings, he "flew swiftly through the stormy reaches of the swirling cosmos, and embraced it all, in the process mating with it." This brought on a flood of light, for the first time illuminating all that existed. The great "cosmic union" effected by Eros made possible the emergence of "divine beings, the infinite heavens, the earth, and the oceans' mighty swells."[8]

Order from Disorder

In fact, the power of love coursing through Eros's vast body made possible the emergence not only of earth, but also all the nonliving and livings things on it. The force of order steadily rippled through Chaos's scrambled matter, causing the heavier elements to sink downward and become the rolling plains, mountains, rivers, and oceans. Above the landmasses loomed the curved canopy of the sky, studded with the slowly moving sun, moon, and stars. Meanwhile, deep beneath earth's illuminated surface lurked the dark underworld, along with its lowest, blackest level, forbidding Tartarus.

When the bright, warm rays of the light that Eros produced touched the surfaces of earth's landed portions, something wonderful occurred. Trees, bushes, flowers, and other plants started to rise upward from the ground and spread slowly but surely across the continents. A similar process was at work in the oceans, as coral reefs and marine plants multiplied in the liquid depths.

The classical Greeks did not envision Eros specifically creating the earth, oceans, and sky. Nor did they think he created the plants on the land and in the seas. Just as the Greek creation myths suggest that the universe itself gave birth to a seed that became the godlike being Eros, the Greeks believed that the seeds of land and ocean plants already existed within Chaos's swirling masses long before Eros appeared.

Moreover, even when Eros entered the picture, he was not a creator deity like God in the Hebrew and Christian creation story. Rather, the power of love within Eros had a natural ability to cause the cosmos's disordered elements to become ordered. Those varied materials came together and fell into tidy, logical categories and niches. It also seemed logical that those niches within nature's fabric would grow more complex over time. This is why Greek thinkers like Plato and Aristotle felt they could explain why nature appeared to be so well thought out and intricate, even though no thinking being had created it all.

Thus, the classical Greeks' vision of the creation, which derived from their ancient myths, was in essence more mechanical and scientific than spiritual. That fact had a crucial effect on the evolution of the Greeks' view of the world, life, and humanity's place in the greater scheme of things. Little more than a century after Hesiod's time, Greek thinkers like Thales and Anaximander introduced the world's first scientific ideas and principles. These early philosopher-scientists speculated that natural laws somehow built *into* nature, not supernatural beings existing *beyond* nature, made the cosmos operate. In this way, the Greek creation myths directly contributed to the rise of science in Western civilization.

Plato on the Creation

Indeed, beginning with Thales, who was born in the late 600s BCE, a long series of early Greek scientists tried to describe how the cosmos began and what it was made of. This made them in a sense the world's first true astronomers. Their starting point was the creation myth involving Chaos and Eros as told by Hesiod and some other early poets. Unlike many less-educated Greeks, who saw that tale as more or less true, Thales and his colleagues recognized it was only a fable. Yet their contention was that such folktales handed down from generation to generation were likely based in part on real events. Therefore, they reasoned, the creation myth told by Hesiod might be an imprecise, garbled version of what really happened.

The first of that series of early Greek astronomers to hit on a vision of the cosmos's creation that was fairly close to the version accepted by modern science was Plato. Born in Athens in 424 BCE, he studied and wrote about a wide range of subjects, among them ethics, politics, the law, and astronomy. Relating to his investigations into the cosmos's origins, his main work was the *Timaeus*, completed around 360 BCE. It presented the world's first comprehensive cosmology, that is, a detailed explanation of how the universe came to be, along with its physical form and workings. The modern science of cosmology was, conceptually speaking, based in large part on Plato's version.

Today's cosmologists think that every particle of matter that exists in the present universe appeared in a monstrous explosion they call the "big bang." In contrast, Plato was less sure of how the cosmos began. He was willing to accept that one key element of the Greek creation myth—Chaos—once existed. But where had Chaos itself come from, he quite logically wondered? In fact, the first major question he posed in the *Timaeus* was whether the universe was "always in existence and without beginning," or instead, "had it a beginning?"[9]

Similarly, even if the cosmos did have a creator, Plato reasoned, one would have to explain where that superior being had originated. But such a "maker of all this universe is past finding out," he wrote. "And even if we found him, to tell of him to all men would be impossible."[10] Therefore, Plato ultimately concluded, it was beyond the mental powers of human beings to discover exactly how the cosmos formed.

Relying on his studies of the cosmos, the early Greek astronomer Plato (center, left) tried to explain the origins of the universe. He nevertheless believed that human beings were incapable of understanding exactly how the cosmos formed.

How Gaea Comforted Sick People

Gaea's association with the oracle at Delphi was not her only role in classical Greek worship. The Greeks also fashioned statues and altars in her honor and prayed to her. Often this adoration took place alongside worship of Demeter, a major agricultural goddess whose primary symbol was a sheaf of wheat. The Greeks also sometimes looked on Demeter as a kind of deity of the earth, as Gaea was. In his now famous guidebook, the second-century-CE Greek traveler Pausanias told about a shrine at Patrai, in southern Greece, that was built in honor of both goddesses. In his words, the residents of the town had "a sacred grove beside the sea" that was "a delightful place for [strolling and sitting] in the summer. In this wood there are some shrines" and statues of Demeter, her daughter Persephone, and the elderly earth deity Gaea. Pausanias added that "the statue of Gaea is sitting down. There is a spring in front of the sanctuary with a dry stone wall on the temple side and a way down to the spring on the outer side." Pausanias also explained that people who were ill often arrived at the shrine hoping that Gaea and Demeter would comfort them. In particular, it was thought those deities might reveal whether or not the illnesses in question were life threatening.

Pausanias, *Guide to Greece,* vol. 1, trans. Peter Levi. New York: Penguin, 1971, pp. 283–84.

Plato's observations of the early cosmos did conform in some ways to the tale told in the myth. That story envisioned the creation as happening in stages—the first one being when Night and Erebus separated and became distinct from Chaos. Then those primitive beings gave rise to a cosmic egg, which hatched to produce Eros; over time Eros made it possible for other seeds inherent in Chaos to separate out and achieve a state of order. To Plato, this suggested that the creation was to some degree an ongoing process. "All sensible things," he said, "are in a process of creation,"[11] whether by their own motivation or by the hand of a creator.

The Ultimate Parents

The idea of creation motivated randomly by the things created, rather than by an intelligent designer, is also evident in the next section of the creation myth told by Hesiod. After the presence of Eros allowed order to replace disorder in the infant cosmos, two more godlike beings emerged. More precisely, their vast bodies already existed, but they now awakened, for the first time gaining a conscious state. One was Gaea (or Gaia). The personification of, or living spirit within, earth's landforms, the Greeks came to call her Mother Earth. Because she supposedly inhabited the ground, they believed she was aware of all that happened among the people and animals connected to the earth's surface.

The other massive spirit that awakened was Uranus, who embodied the sky floating above the earth. He became known to the later Greeks, appropriately, as Father Heaven. There were different accounts of where he came from. Hesiod's was the most prominent; he wrote that Gaea "bore starry Heaven, first to be an equal to herself, to cover her all over, and to be a resting-place, always secure, for all the blessed gods."[12] (Other ancient accounts claimed that Uranus came into being of his own accord or was the son of Night.)

These myths of the emergence of Gaea and Uranus had a potent effect on the evolution of the religious customs of the later classical Greeks. First, they believed that Mother Earth possessed the power of prophecy, or foretelling future events. Partly for that reason, they often connected her with the renowned oracle at Delphi, in central Greece. An oracle was a place—usually a temple or shrine—that people visited in hopes of learning about the future. The term *oracle* also referred to the prophecy itself and to the priestess who spoke it, supposedly on behalf of a god.

WORD ORIGINS

oracle

In ancient Greece: a shrine to which religious pilgrims journeyed to hear divine revelations about the future.

In modern life: a person who knows an unusually large number of facts.

According to one ancient tradition, Gaea was the first deity to erect a temple at Delphi. To guard the area, she installed a very large snake, named Python, who killed and ate anyone whom the goddess had not invited. Eventually, the story went, the young god Apollo came by, slew Python, and seized control of Delphi. Well aware that he was taking something that belonged to the earth mother, he pacified her by founding a series of yearly poetry and sports contests in her honor. (They became known as the Pythian Games, after the Pythia, the title assumed by each of the priestesses in the local temple.)

WORD ORIGINS

Python

In ancient Greece: the huge serpent that guarded Gaea's shrine at Delphi.

In modern life: python, a large snake that uses its body to crush its prey.

Another aspect of later Greek religious and social customs influenced by the early myths about Gaea and Uranus was based on the concept that these beings were fundamental parental figures. Most Greeks greatly respected their parents, and it was not unusual to make a promise and swear to keep it on the life of one's father or mother. Similarly, Gaea and Uranus were widely seen as the ultimate keepers of oaths, or solemn promises. Therefore, it was also common to swear by one or both of those primeval deities.

That custom of swearing by Gaea and/or Uranus is illustrated in a number of surviving classical Greek literary works. One is the *Argonautica* ("Voyage of the Argo"), written by the third-century-BCE Greek Apollonius of Rhodes. At one point, a woman urges her sister to "swear by Gaea and Uranus that you will keep what I say to yourself and work in league with me." The sister assures her, "I will do as you ask and take the solemn oath of the Colkians, swearing by mighty Uranus and by Gaea below, the Mother of the Gods."[13]

A Glutton for Creating Offspring

Another important aspect of the myths surrounding Gaea and Uranus was that they were not parents merely in the symbolic, or figurative, sense. The two huge beings actually mated, over time producing many offspring. A majority of them were seen by the classical Greeks and other later peoples as monsters. For example, three of them possessed fifty heads and one hundred hands each. Their parents named them

Gyas, Cottos, and Braireos. Another three gruesome creatures sired by Gaea and Uranus were the Cyclopes (SY-cloh-peez), a Greek word meaning "wheel-eyed." This name derived from the disturbing fact that each had one big, glaring eye in the middle of his forehead.

According to the myth, even when Uranus was not around, Gaea kept busy producing more children. She was said to have somehow given birth on her own to a sea god named Pontus, who personified

Until it was slain by the god Apollo, the mythological serpent called Python guarded Gaea's temple at Delphi. To blunt Gaea's anger at the creature's death, Apollo founded a series of yearly poetry and sports contests in her honor.

"the barren sea with its swollen waves,"[14] according to Hesiod. Not long after that, the mother and her new son proceeded to mate. This weird union gave rise to a large number of sea gods, including Ceto, Phorcys, Nereus, Eurynia, and Thaumus.

A veritable glutton for creating offspring, Gaea next mated with Tartarus, the deepest, scariest level of the dim underworld. Perhaps because Tartarus itself was so dark and creepy, its child with Gaea—Echidna—was a hideous beast. Ancient accounts describe it as half serpent, half woman, and all repulsive.

WORD ORIGINS

theoi

In ancient Greece: the word for gods.

In modern life: theology, the study of religion.

After giving birth to so many frightening creatures, Gaea was dissatisfied. Surely, she told herself, she could muster the strength to produce a brood of more handsome beings. So she once more coupled with Uranus and this time concentrated all her energies on making babies with attractive features. The result was the emergence of what the classical Greeks viewed as the first true race of gods, or *theoi*, who were themselves destined to carry the process of creation to bold new levels.

Chapter Two

The Rise of the Titans

Although Gaea and Uranus produced many offspring, their most famous and important children were the Titans, who made up the first race of gods recognized by the later classical Greeks. Unlike most of the earlier monstrous creatures the earth mother and sky father generated, the Titans looked "normal" by human standards. That is, each had a single head, two arms, two legs, and two eyes.

Yet although the Titans *looked* like the humans who would appear in a later stage of the creation, they were far from human in several other ways. First, the Titans were what the Greeks called *gigantes*, or giants. The typical Titan stood at least 25 feet (7.6 m) high, about five times taller than the average person.

The members of the first race of gods were also significantly more powerful than humans. Not only did they have more muscular strength than people do, the Titans also possessed special divine powers that humans lack. With occasional exceptions, these special abilities were connected to the workings of the cosmos. For instance, some Titans were responsible for maintaining the world's physical integrity—like helping to keep the vast bodies of their parents, the earth and sky, firmly in place. In their art the classical Greeks sometimes pictured four Titans acting as large-scale cosmic pillars holding the sky in place above the earth. In the east stood mighty Hyperion; in the west was equally powerful Iapetos; meanwhile, Coeus held up the sky in the north; and Crius did the same in the south.

Hesiod affirmed these gods' powers. He also described how the chief Titan, Cronos, and some of his fellow gods sometimes stood in the center of the world. There, it was said, they maintained the orderly passage of time and regular heavenly cycles. Meanwhile, Coeus, who held up the sky's northern section, also made sure that the constellations, the groups of stars seen in the night sky, slowly moved in a great circle far above earth.

WORD ORIGINS

gigantes

In ancient Greece: the word for giants.

In modern life: gigantic.

Among the various mythical traditions revolving around the Titans was one originally popular in Crete, the large Greek island bordering the southern Aegean Sea. It held that the age in which these early deities ruled the universe was, from a material standpoint, a sort of golden age. In those days, the story went, the soil produced a seemingly endless amount of food. For that reason, classical Greek art contains many images of Titans holding sickles and other farm implements.

The Leading Titans

Although hundreds of Titans existed, a relative few were the strongest, and it was only natural that they usually led, outperformed, or overshadowed the others. The strongest Titan of all, Cronos, assumed the role of king of the gods. Part of the reason for his supremacy was that he frequently threw his weight around. A big, mean-spirited, violent lout, he often bullied the other Titans into submission. His sister, Rhea, a goddess who kept the soil fertile, did not like or want to marry him, for instance. But he forced her into it.

Next to Cronos and Rhea, perhaps the most famous and important of the early Titans was Oceanus. He was the deity personifying the large freshwater river—or Ocean—that the classical Greeks envisioned as encircling the world's land portions. They also associated this supposedly strong and always-flowing stream of water with the never-ending flow of time. Another aspect of Oceanus's unusually potent power was the influence he had over the cosmic, or heavenly, bodies—the sun, moon, and stars. He made sure that they rose and set on a regular schedule.

Oceanus (left) personified the large freshwater river that the ancient Greeks believed encircled the world. After the emergence of the Titans, Oceanus seized control of all the waters of the world, aided by his wife Tethys (right).

Moreover, the creation myths and other tales featuring Oceanus strongly influenced the way the classical Greeks saw a particular geographic aspect of their world—the way in which water was distributed. Every Greek child knew the story of how, after the emergence of the Titans, Oceanus seized control of all the waters in the world. In addition to the vast, more or less circular outer ocean, he held sway over every river, stream, and rain-filled cloud, along with the wells later created by people. His wife—another influential Titan named Tethys—helped him with this huge job. She used her strong will to push some of the world's water through the enormous caves that this and other myths claimed existed deep underground.

Oceanus was a character in many other Greek myths as well, and numerous Greek literary works mentioned his exploits. One of the best-known examples appears in the *Iliad*. That renowned epic poem is credited to the classical Greeks' favorite poet, Homer, who is thought to have lived in the 700s BCE. In the passage in question, the bold and skilled Greek warrior Achilles is challenged by a man who says he possesses the power of one of Oceanus's swift-flowing rivers. In the ensuing fight, Achilles is the victor. Standing over the body, he mocks the idea that the Titan god of the waters could stand up to his own divine patron—Zeus. "All the world's rivers, and the seas, too, along with all the world's streams and deep wells, flow directly through Oceanus," Achilles admits. "Yet even mighty Oceanus fears the lightning and awful thunderbolt of the great Zeus when he shakes the skies with his loud crashes."[15]

WORD ORIGINS

Oceanus

In ancient Greece: the Titan in charge of the seas, rivers, streams, and other bodies of water.

In modern life: ocean.

Homer's *Iliad* was a staple of education in classical Greece. Students did more than simply read that great work. They also memorized lengthy excerpts of the text and frequently were able to recite them word for word for the rest of their life. As a result, the mythical tales involving Oceanus and other Titans were perpetuated over the generations.

Atlas, the Living Pillar

The classical Greeks also enjoyed learning about the mythical exploits of other Titans. Not all of these deities fostered extensive separate myths of their own, however. Some of them were known to the Greeks mainly through brief mentions in the stories about more famous Titans. Perses, for example, was one of these minor Titans about whom little is known. He was mentioned briefly in a few ancient accounts as a destroyer god and/or a deity who brought summer droughts. His daughter, Hecate, who was also rarely mentioned in myths, had a reputation as a dabbler in witchcraft.

In contrast, several of the Titans were very well known to and popular with the ancient Greeks. One was Atlas, who was associated with movement of constellations through the night sky. Some ancient traditions claimed Atlas was the god of astronomy. As the son of the Titan Iapetos, who helped hold up the sky, it was not surprising that Atlas also became known for supporting the heavens.

How the Atlas Mountains Came to Be

The best-known myth about Atlas is the one in which the Titan met and interacted with the renowned Greek strongman Heracles. But another mythical tale about Atlas was almost as famous. In it, a different Greek hero, Perseus, traveled through North Africa and met up with the Titan who held up part of the sky. Not long before this fateful meeting, Perseus had slain a hideous female monster named Medusa. According to legend, she was so horrifying that people and animals who gazed on her instantly turned to stone. Perseus managed to avoid that fate by looking at Medusa's reflection in a polished shield, rather than directly at her, while killing her. When Perseus approached Atlas, he was carrying Medusa's head in a bag. The Titan had earlier been warned that a young Greek would soon arrive and try to steal the golden apples belonging to Atlas's daughters, the Hesperides. So the giant god tried to drive Perseus away. Upset over this poor show of hospitality, Perseus reached into the bag and pulled out Medusa's severed head. Unfortunately for Atlas, he stared right at the gruesome artifact and as a result rapidly turned to stone. Many classical Greeks believed that this myth explained how the Atlas Mountains, situated in northwestern Africa, came to be.

In fact, the most famous mythical tradition related to Atlas said that he used his immense strength to hold up the sky and keep it from crashing onto earth. The frequent modern depictions of him holding the globe-like earth on his back are inaccurate. It was the sky sphere, *not* the world sphere, that he bore on his back in his chief myth.

That tale also involved the renowned Greek strongman Heracles, (whom the Romans later called Hercules). A Greek king had ordered him to perform twelve labors, each seen as a task too difficult for an ordinary person to do. The eleventh labor consisted of traveling to faraway North Africa and finding the legendary and valuable golden apples belonging to the Hesperides. The latter minor goddesses were Atlas's daughters. This made it quite possible that Heracles might meet up with the well-known Titan during the journey.

Sure enough, one day as he made his way through the North African countryside, Heracles saw a huge human-like figure standing in the distance. When the man got closer, he saw that the figure was the renowned Atlas. The Titan was holding up a large portion of the sky, clearly a difficult and tiring job. After Heracles explained to the god why he had come, Atlas offered to go find his daughters and get the golden apples. All he asked was that the man temporarily stand in for him and hold up the sky until he returned.

Heracles, who was also renowned for his great strength, did as the god said and began supporting a hefty portion of the heavens. When Atlas returned with the treasure, however, he refused to resume the tedious task he had long undertaken. The man was stuck with that heavy chore forever, he said with a smile. Fortunately for Heracles, he was smarter than Atlas. Heracles said he badly needed to change the way the sky's bulk pressed on his shoulders and persuaded the Titan to support the heavens for a moment while he made the adjustment. At the last moment, however, the man slipped away, leaving Atlas once more as a living pillar between earth and sky.

WORD ORIGINS

Titan

In ancient Greece: a member of the first race of Greek gods, each of whom was huge.

In modern life: titanic, meaning extremely large.

Inspiration for Greek Artists

This myth about Atlas and his tiresome task had a potent influence on the art of the classical Greeks. Some of the artists who depicted scenes from the story were painters. A later Greek traveler, Pausanias, mentioned a vivid painting depicting such a scene on one side of a large treasure chest he saw at Olympia. Located in southwestern Greece, Olympia was the site of the famous sporting contests known as the Olympic Games. Describing the painting and the caption carved beneath it, both now lost, Pausanias wrote, "Atlas too is

Atlas bears the weight of the sky on his shoulders to keep it from crashing into the earth. The Titan briefly escaped his burden but ultimately was forced once again to stand as a living pillar between earth and sky.

supporting [the sky], just as the story has it, upon his shoulders. He is also carrying the apples of the Hesperides. A man holding a sword is coming towards Atlas. This everybody can see is Heracles, though he is not mentioned specifically in the caption, which reads: 'Here is Atlas holding up heaven, but he will let go the apples.'"[16]

"Her Rays Beam Clear"

A few classical Greek writers composed hymns dedicated to some of the oldest race of gods—the Titans. The Greeks recited hymns in various situations, some strictly religious, others artistic in nature. Some hymns were meant to be spoken or sung at festivals in which speakers held contests to see who could recite epic poems the best. Just before the formal contest began, someone recited a hymn to honor the deity to whom the competition was dedicated. In this case the hymn honored Selene, the Titan goddess of the moon.

> From her immortal head a radiance is shown from heaven and embraces earth. And great is the beauty that arises from her shining light. The air, unlit before, glows with the light of her golden crown, and her rays beam clear, whenever bright Selene, having bathed her lovely body in the waters of [the Titan] Oceanus, and dons her far-gleaming raiment [dress]. She yokes her strong-necked, shining [chariot] team, and drives on her long-haired horses at full speed in the mid-month. Then her great orbit is full and then her beams shine brightest as she increases [in brightness]. So she is a sure sign to mortal men. . . . Hail, white-armed goddess, bright Selene, mild, bright-haired queen! And now I will leave you and sing the glories of men half-divine, whose deeds minstrels celebrate with lovely lips.

Homeric Hymn No. 32, in *Hesiod, The Homeric Hymns, and Homerica,* trans. H.G. Evelyn-White. Cambridge, MA: Harvard University Press, 1964, pp. 459, 461.

Another aspect of Greek art strongly influenced by Atlas's main myth was sculpture. Sometime in the third century BCE, an unknown Greek sculptor completed a magnificent statue of the mighty Titan standing 7 feet (2 m) tall. The work showed Atlas kneeling and holding on his back a large sky sphere bearing most of the constellations then known to Greek astronomers.

Not long after it was created, that sculpture disappeared, possibly stolen during the Roman invasion of Greece in the following century. Before it was lost, however, a Roman sculptor copied the Greek original. (The Roman copy has survived. Called the Farnese Atlas, it rests in the National Archaeological Museum in Naples, on Italy's western coast.) The original version of the statue was only one of many ancient Greek artistic renderings of the Titans. They demonstrated how both artists and the public that admired their works were inspired and entertained by dramatic scenes from mythology.

Cronos Versus Uranus

Besides Atlas, several other Titans appeared in both major and minor creation myths perpetuated by the classical Greeks in their art. Some were clearly associated with the foundation of the regular daily operations of nature and the cosmos, a theme common among the Titans' tales. Typical of these beings was Eos, goddess of the dawn (also seen as the mother deity of the planets that moved among the stars). The Greeks pictured her as rising up from the horizon and into the sky each day, sometimes riding in a golden chariot drawn by winged horses. Other Greek artistic renderings showed her moving through the air via a splendid pair of wings.

Similarly, Eos's brother Titan, Helios, was god of the sun. That radiant deity was thought to reside in a golden palace situated just below the far eastern horizon. Each day he supposedly left that home base riding a chariot drawn by four winged horses surrounded by a brilliant, almost blinding burst of sunlight. Later, after disappearing in the west at day's close, Helios returned to his palace to rest and prepare for the following day's ride.

Of all the Titans, however, none was depicted as often in classical Greek literature and art as the king of those early deities—Cronos.

> # WORD ORIGINS
>
> ## Helios
>
> In ancient Greece: the Titan god of the sun.
>
> In modern life: heliocentric, describing the theory that the sun is the center of the solar system.

Helios, god of the sun, rides toward the horizon in his horse-drawn chariot. His daily ride filled the sky with bright sunlight.

This may be partly attributed to his key role in two major myths. In the first, he attacked his own father, Uranus. Somewhat dim-witted and suspicious of everyone, Uranus worried that his more monstrous children, like those with one hundred hands, might attack him. So one by one he ambushed, captured, and imprisoned them in the dark depths of Tartarus.

Gaea loved all her children, so she was outraged at what Uranus had done. According to Hesiod, she said to Cronos, "If you will obey me, we should punish the vile outrage of your father." Cronos answered, "Mother, I will undertake to do this deed," and he eagerly grasped a sharp farmer's sickle that she handed him. Soon, arrogant Uranus walked by, and "the son from his ambush stretched forth his left hand and in his right took the great long sickle."[17] In one swift stroke, Cronos sliced off his father's genitals, which fell bleeding to the ground. Then the younger god cast the badly injured Uranus into Tartarus.

Rhea's Ruse

The other major creation myth about Cronos that the Greeks frequently retold provided the background events for the ultimate downfall of the once glorious race of Titans. After eliminating his father, the story went, Cronos proceeded to have children with his wife, Rhea. However, just before the birth of the first infant, the leading Titan became worried. Would his own offspring turn on him, he wondered, as he had betrayed his own father, Uranus?

To keep such an event from happening, Cronos waited till the first child was born and then grabbed and swallowed it whole. (The baby did not perish, because it was immortal, like the other gods. Trapped inside its parent's belly, in the years that followed it continued to grow.) In the same way, Cronos went on to gulp down the next four children born to Rhea.

No less than Gaea did, Rhea cared deeply for her children. So when she was ready to have her sixth baby, she decided to save it by fooling Cronos. As the child was born, she stealthily hid it and in its place handed her husband a stone wrapped in a blanket. Almost as mentally dense as his own father, Cronos did not detect the ruse and hastily swallowed the stone, thinking it was his newest offspring.

This grisly but compelling tale had a direct impact on the classical Greeks. Sometime in the seventh or sixth century BCE, someone living in Delphi discovered a stone that local priests declared to be the very one that Rhea had long ago handed to Cronos. The locals named it the Omphalos, meaning "navel," and put it on display inside a temple in the sprawling religious complex at Delphi. For many centuries, people came from far and wide to glimpse the relic. One of them was Pausanias, who described it as a white marble orb that the Delphians claimed to be "the center of the entire earth."[18]

For most classical Greeks, creation myths and reality seemed to merge in the Delphian navel stone. If that old tale was more or less true, the common wisdom went, other creation myths might also be based on fact. In particular, people wanted to know how the principal gods they worshipped—those said to dwell atop Mount Olympus— had originated. For that epic tale, the Greeks picked up where the story of Cronos swallowing his children left off. Everyone knew that the sixth infant—the one Rhea had rescued—was none other than Zeus, who was destined to establish a new and truly fabulous race of gods.

Chapter Three

<hr/>

The Olympians
Take Charge

After the rise and reign of the Titans, the next important episode among the ancient Greek creation myths addressed the appearance of the main gods worshipped by the classical Greeks. These deities, who ended up replacing the Titans as controllers of the cosmos, were often called the Olympians. This was a reference to a folktale that claimed they lived at the summit of Greece's highest peak, Mount Olympus.

As creation tales went, the origins of the Olympian gods and formation of their society were particularly vital to the ancient Greeks. This was partly because most Greeks were quite devout in their worship of these deities. Also, those gods and the myths and rites associated with them were unifying forces among all Greeks. No matter what their political and cultural differences might be at any given time, they worshipped the same deities in the same manner and recognized the same myths.

Moreover, the myths of the Olympians' origins made it clear that those beings were in many ways closely related to people. Each deity not only looked like an *anthropos*, Greek for "human being," but also displayed human emotions and made mistakes like people do. Thus, the Olympians were not morally perfect, as the supreme being of the Jews, Christians, and Muslims is said to be.

Nevertheless, as their exploits in the creation myths showed, the Olympian gods *had* to be respected at all costs. First, they were immortal, which meant they would live forever. Second, they possessed powers and abilities far beyond those of mortal humans. The great early Greek poet Homer made that clear in his epic the *Iliad*. (That work, along with his other epic, the *Odyssey*, contains crucial descriptions of the gods, depictions that strongly shaped Greek views of those deities.) Indeed, over and over, Homer made it clear that humans could never compare to the gods. In the *Iliad*, one of the Olympians, Apollo, warns the conceited Greek warrior Diomedes, "Never try to claim you are the same as the gods, who are immortal, for men, who walk on the ground, can never be their equals."[19]

In the Caves of Crete

The mythical story of how the Olympians came to be begins partway through the tale of how Cronos, the brutish king of the Titans, swallowed each of his six children birthed by his wife, Rhea. At least that is how Cronos saw it. In truth, Rhea deceived him by replacing the sixth infant with a stone, which her husband stupidly gulped down. In this way the Titan queen managed to save her last child, Zeus. She ordered her servants to carry him off to the island of Crete, where two minor goddesses secretly cared for him in a cave.

This part of the myth, in which a Cretan cave was a central feature, was both believable and meaningful to the classical Greeks. They had long had literary traditions suggesting that during the long-ago Age of Heroes the inhabitants of Crete both lived and worshipped in caves, which are plentiful on that island. So it made sense that Rhea would have sent the infant Zeus to live in a Cretan cave. There he would have been well protected and well nourished.

As it turns out, modern archaeologists have shown that those traditional classical Greek beliefs about Crete's caves were largely true. During the Bronze Age, the modern designation for what the ancient Greeks called the Age of Heroes, Crete was home to the Minoans. It is now known that the Minoans' ancestors lived in caves. Later, moreover, when the Minoans began dwelling in houses, they transformed

---

WORD ORIGINS

anthropos

In ancient Greece: the word for human being.

In modern life: anthropology, the study of human societies.

The caves of Crete (pictured) provided safety for the young god Zeus, whose siblings had all been swallowed by their father, Cronos. Eventually Zeus freed his brothers and sisters from their father's belly and rose to lead the Olympians.

those caves into both cemeteries and shrines where worship took place. Dim memories of people worshipping gods in Crete's caves survived into classical times. So it is not surprising that those old tales inspired the myth of Zeus spending his childhood in a Cretan cave.

Rescuing His Siblings

The creation myth of the Olympian gods does not specify exactly how long Zeus spent in the cave. Various episodes from the divine child's upbringing appear in several different ancient sources. One, a hymn composed by a classical Greek, states that baby Zeus lay "in a cradle of gold" and for milk "sucked the rich nipple of the she-goat Amalthea" and for food ate "the sweet honey-comb"[20] of bees who fashioned their hives in the foothills of Mount Ida, the tallest peak in Crete.

According to Hesiod, "The strength and glorious limbs of the young lord [Zeus] grew quickly and the years went by."[21] When Rhea's sixth child had at last become an adult, his mother finally told him who his father was and what the king of the Titans had done to Zeus's five siblings. Already a champion of justice, a trait he would thereafter always display, the young deity became determined to free his brothers and sisters from Cronos's bloated belly.

To implement this daring plan, Zeus quietly acquired a small quantity of a potent drug. Traveling in disguise to mainland Greece, he secretly sprinkled some of that medicine into Cronos's dinner, and in less than a minute the huge Titan got green in the face and began vomiting uncontrollably. First he threw up the stone that Rhea had given him in place of Zeus; then, one after another, up came the five long-trapped babies, now grown into adult gods. Hera, protector of women, appeared; and next came Poseidon, god of the seas; Hades, master of the underworld; Demeter, the grain goddess; and Hestia, protector of the hearth.

These rescued deities were pleased to meet Zeus, whom they recognized as their leader. All six agreed that they formed the core of a new race of divinities who should try to overthrow Cronos and his Titan supporters. But first Zeus and his kin took the time to strengthen their ranks. Zeus quickly mated with a Titan named Leto, who gave birth to twin deities—Apollo, soon to be the god of prophecy, and Artemis, who would become goddess of wild animals and hunting.

One particularly powerful new ally for the group was Zeus's daughter Athena, goddess of war and wisdom. According to Hesiod, "Zeus himself gave birth, from his own head, to bright-eyed Athena, the awful [fierce], strife-stirring, the leader, the tireless, the queen who delights in tumults, and wars, and battles."[22]

The Titanomachy Begins

In addition to creating new divine offspring, Zeus managed to convince some of the Titans to join him. Among them were Prometheus, whose name means "seeing beforehand," and his brother, Epimetheus,

---

WORD ORIGINS

Odyssey

In ancient Greece: one of the two grand epic poems credited to the early Greek poet Homer.

In modern life: odyssey, meaning an arduous or time-consuming trip.

Myth-Tellers' Corner: Homer

No one knows exactly when Homer, the ancient Greeks' most beloved poet, was born. Most modern experts think he flourished sometime between 800 and 650 BCE. One of a group of bards who recited long epic poems, essentially detailed stories told in verse, he is credited with creating the final versions of two already existing works. The first, the *Iliad,* describes a series of events near the end of the famous mythical Trojan War; the second epic, the *Odyssey,* covers the exploits of Odysseus, one of the Greek kings who fought in that conflict.

Another important mystery surrounding Homer is whether he actually composed, or at least tweaked and finished, both epics. Some scholars think he might have composed or finalized only one of them, and a few suggest someone else wrote both works. Attempts to answer such questions are part of a still-ongoing subject of debate usually referred to as the "Homeric question." In reality, it consists of several questions, including where he was born, if he was even a real person, and if the incidents described in the epics were imaginary or based on real events.

Nevertheless, the vast majority of historians are convinced that Homer was a real person who brought both epics to their magnificent final literary states. Those works—chock-full of crucial myths— exerted a profound influence on Greek culture and thought. They gave the classical Greeks much practical wisdom and a virtual blueprint for a righteous code of conduct.

or "seeing only afterward." Prometheus was the chief character in *Prometheus Bound,* penned by the great fifth-century-BCE Athenian playwright Aeschylus, who based the work on the creation myth of the Olympians. In the play, Prometheus explains how he got involved in the dispute between the two divine races. "When first among the immortal gods anger broke out, dividing them into factions," he recalls, Zeus and his allies "resolved to unseat the power of Cronos, and make Zeus absolute king." Meanwhile, "the opposing side resolved no less that Zeus should never rule the gods. At that time, I, offering the best of all advice, tried to convince the Titan sons of Heaven and Earth"[23] not to resort to violence.

According to Hesiod, Athena—goddess of war and wisdom—sprang from the head of Zeus. She became a powerful ally of Zeus and the namesake of the great Greek city-state of Athens.

But this peaceful approach failed, Prometheus goes on, because most of the Titans "despised cunning. In their pride of strength, they foresaw easy victory and the rule of might." Possessing the gift of forethought,

> I knew the appointed course of things to come. My mother [the Titan Themis] had many times foretold to me that not brute strength, not violence, but instead cunning must give victory to the rulers of the future. This I explained to [the war-mongering Titans], which they found not worth one moment's heed. Then, of the courses open to me, it seemed best to take my stand—my mother with me—at the side of Zeus.[24]

The fact that Prometheus attempted to use diplomacy to avoid bloodshed on both sides demonstrates how the classical Greeks envisioned wars among the city-states. But it is not certain that the episode involving diplomacy was part of the original tale. Aeschylus may have inserted that part in an effort to show that the gods were as sophisticated in matters of war and peace as were the classical Greeks. Indeed, the Greeks knew well how devastating war could be. When possible, therefore, they usually tried to avoid it. Their creation myths, which apparently were still being shaped and reshaped in Aeschylus's day, reflected this fact.

Returning to the myth, as Zeus's fledgling army continued to grow, slow-witted Cronos finally took notice and began to worry. The blundering but brawny Titan hurried to and fro, gathering his own followers and warning them that they must capture and imprison Zeus and his newly created deities. Otherwise, the Titans might lose their place as masters of the universe. (Cronos did not suggest killing his opponents, because he realized they were, like him, immortal and therefore could not be slain.)

When the two armies finally faced off and went on the attack, earth and the heavens became embroiled in a huge, furious battle. The classical Greeks called it the Titanomachy, or "War of the Titans." Day after day, year after year, without a single break, the combatants raged against one another with all their might.

The Female Olympians

Among the Olympians, the new race of gods largely created or brought together by Zeus, were five female deities who were avidly worshipped by the classical Greeks. Hera, Zeus's sister and wife, was seen as a protector of married women and the marriage institution itself. Her primary symbol was the peacock. Another female divinity in the Olympian camp was Zeus's daughter Athena, a deity of war who was also known for her wisdom and as a protector of civilized life. Her namesake, Athens, became Greece's most populous and influential city. Artemis, twin sister of Apollo, god of prophecy, oversaw wild lands and animals, the moon, and hunting, and also protected young girls.

Meanwhile, the female deity Demeter was in charge of agriculture, particularly the growing of wheat and other grains, which explains why her main symbol was a sheaf of wheat. Her sister Hestia was the champion and protector of the hearth, the fireplace that existed in every Greek home. The hearth not only allowed people to cook their food but also was a place for family members to gather. Most Greeks began their meals with a prayer to Hestia. The final female Olympian was the striking and elegant Aphrodite, goddess of love. She was said to have risen from a collection of bubbling sea foam to become a much-respected, though often jealous, divine being. Her symbols were the rose and the dove.

Zeus's New Advantages

During the incredible battle, the members of the opposing divine races used every means at their disposal to gain the upper hand. Some uprooted large trees and used them as clubs. Others grasped enormous boulders and hurled them miles into the air. Meanwhile, some of the sea gods marshaled the forces of giant waves, crashing them down onto enemies standing near the shores.

The seemingly relentless conflict dragged on for ten years, until finally one god had an idea for how to ensure victory for his side. The insightful Prometheus, still fighting for Zeus, realized that no one was utilizing a tremendous potential military asset. Namely, several of the strongest, fiercest fighters in existence—the giant Cyclopes and monstrous beasts with one hundred hands—were still languishing in dark Tartarus. Those frightening creatures despised Cronos, Prometheus told Zeus. So they would almost certainly want to oppose the Titans.

In his battle for dominance among the gods, Zeus enlisted the help of the enormous one-eyed creatures known as Cyclopes. Freed from their underworld prison, they immediately set about creating huge thunderbolts for Zeus.

Hearing this advice, Zeus hurried down into the shadowy under-world and soon reached the enormous stone doors leading to Tartarus. Using one of his powerful thunderbolts to break the lock, he released the three largest Cyclopes—Lightener, Thunderer, and Shiner by name. Thankful for their freedom, they immediately went to work creating the biggest thunderbolts ever seen for Zeus. They also fashioned a three-pronged spear, called a trident, for Poseidon and a unique cap for Hades that made him invisible when he wore it. Zeus also released the so-called Hundred-Handers. Unlike the Titans, who were limited to throwing one rock or spear at a time, these terrifying beings could fling one hundred missiles at once.

Now, with Zeus's army in possession of these new advantages, the war resumed and became more devastating than ever. "The boundless sea rang terribly around and the earth crashed loudly," in Hesiod's words. "Wide Heaven was shaken and groaned, and high Olympus reeled from its foundation under the charge of the undying gods, and a heavy quaking reached dim Tartarus and the deep sound of their feet in the fearful onset of their hard missiles. So then, they launched their grievous shafts upon one another, and the cry of both armies as they shouted reached to starry heaven."[25]

Next, Hesiod continued, Zeus, his heart filled with fury, showed why he deserved to be leader of the gods. He rushed down "from heaven and from Olympus," hurling jagged pieces of lightning as he went. "The bolts flew thick and fast," and "the life-giving earth crashed around" and burned, "and the vast forests crackled loud with fire all about."[26]

Dwellers on Olympus?

In the end Cronos and the Titans who fought for him were so badly weakened that Zeus and his own followers were able to defeat and capture them. According to Hesiod, the winners confined the losers to Tartarus in "everlasting shade." Moreover, "they bound them up in painful chains." Zeus ordained that "they may never leave. Poseidon set bronze gates upon the place." Three of the scary giant monsters whom Zeus had recently freed remained beside the gates "as faithful guards."[27]

Having eliminated most of the Titans, Zeus and his followers took charge of the world and started rebuilding the many sections that had been damaged in the war. During these renovations, the new race of gods built several splendid palaces on the summit of Mount Olympus. Thereafter, as a result, they were frequently referred to as the Olympians. (A handful of these deities did not stay on Olympus. For instance, Hades became the master of the underworld and erected his own palace there.)

Besides Zeus and Hades, the later classical Greeks recognized several other powerful deities as members of the original group of Olympians. Zeus's brother Poseidon, the main sea god, was one, and Zeus's wife, Hera, who protected women, was another. There was also Zeus's son Ares, the god of war. Some of the others included the versatile Apollo, lord of prophecy, healing, and music; another son of Zeus, Dionysus, who ensured the soil was fertile and wine was plentiful; and Hephaestus, who served as blacksmith to the gods.

Modern scholars are not sure when the idea that these gods dwelled atop Mount Olympus took hold among the Greeks. The best estimate is that this notion evolved during the cultural dark age that followed the collapse of Greece's Bronze Age society. This belief was no longer the common wisdom in the later classical era, however. By the time of Athens's golden age in the fifth century BCE, it had become a quaint old folktale that few accepted as real. Instead, most Greeks had by now concluded that the gods lived in some unknown quarter of the sky.

In fact, one of the philosophical schools that arose late in classical times took this concept a step further. The Epicureans, followers of the philosopher Epicurus (circa 341–270 BCE), held that the gods might not exist at all. Even if there *were* such deities, Epicurus argued, they likely dwelled far from earth and paid no attention at all to people and their petty problems. If the gods did exist in that manner, the Epicureans suggested, then the events described in the Greek creation myths may once have happened; but those stories were no longer relevant. Most Greeks did not follow Epicurus's teachings, however. So the creation stories, including those involving the Olympians' rise, remained popular and later passed on through the generations across Europe and well beyond.

WORD ORIGINS

Epicurus

In ancient Greece: a fourth-century-BCE Greek thinker who taught that to be happy people should seek pleasure and avoid fear and pain.

In modern life: epicurean (or epicure), meaning someone given to self-indulgence and pleasure-seeking.

Chapter Four

Crafting the Human Race

The classical Greeks were fascinated by their myths that told how the universe emerged from a chaotic jumble of swirling materials. They also cherished and perpetuated their tales of the emergence of the lumbering Titans and the origins of the resourceful Olympian gods they regularly worshipped. Yet none of the Greeks' creation myths held them spellbound more than those that detailed the manner in which humans came to be.

Most peoples and religions have a single creation story. Typically, it tells not only how the cosmos originated, but also how people entered the picture. The shared creation tale of the Jews, Christians, and Muslims, in which God fashioned the world and people in the space of a few days, is a familiar example.

In contrast, the Greeks had several different stories that accounted for the appearance of the human race. Of the two principal tales, one describes how the Greek gods crafted a series of five human races. In the other major version of human origins, a single deity generated people. In his sad but stirring story, he came to cherish them and ended up paying an awful price for his heroic efforts to ensure their survival.

From Gold to Silver

The ancient Greek tradition that envisioned a series of separate human creations held that the Titans were responsible for fashioning the first people. A number of ancient accounts said that Cronos accomplished this feat, making sure to construct those much smaller beings in his own physical image. Other ancient writers suggested that Cronos *ordered* the creation of humans and that other Titans actually carried it out.

In whatever manner these bursts of creation were initiated, together they are frequently called the Five Ages of Men. The first was appropriately called the Age of Gold, or golden age, because it was a time in which people lived in perpetual springtime, never knew poverty, and were supremely happy. Hesiod described that fabulous era in his minor epic poem *Works and Days*. "They lived like gods," he explained,

> without sorrow of heart, remote and free from toil and grief. Miserable aging rested not on them. But with legs and arms never failing, they made merry with feasting beyond the reach of all evils. When they died, it was as though they were overcome with sleep, and they had all good things, for the fruitful earth [generously] bore them fruit abundantly. They dwelt in ease and peace upon their lands with many good things, rich in flocks and loved by the blessed gods.[28]

According to Hesiod and other ancient writers, when Zeus and his Olympians defeated the Titans, Cronos ended up in dark Tartarus. So he could no longer watch over the people who had long lived almost ideal lives. As a result, they disappeared from the scene, and the new rulers of the cosmos replaced them with a less fortunate race of humans, whose time period became known as the Age of Silver.

In that second human era, it was no longer always springtime, nor was a rich bounty of food always available. Instead, the seasons changed and people had to grow their own food. That meant it was necessary for them to work for a living. Also, when winter came the weather grew cold, forcing them to erect houses where they could stay warm.

Another drawback was that these people, in Hesiod's words, were unable to "keep from sinning and from wronging one another. Nor would they serve the immortals, nor sacrifice on the holy altars of the blessed ones as it is right for men to do." This lack of proper reverence for the gods turned out to be the undoing of the residents of the second age. "Zeus," Hesiod said, "was angry" and destroyed them "because they would not give honor to the blessed gods who live on Olympus."[29]

Society's Decline Inevitable?

The idea that humanity had once lived in a golden age of prosperity and later steadily deteriorated seemed to the classical Greeks to be supported by both verbal traditions and physical evidence. First, in addition to the creation tales, many other myths mentioned splendid kingdoms that had existed in past ages. Some, supposedly, had been ruled by fair and just rulers whose subjects were well fed and happy.

Furthermore, during classical times Greece's landscape was dotted with the ruins of once huge and magnificent palaces and fortresses.

In Greek mythology, the first race of humans lived a happy existence—free from work, hunger, and grief. The second race of humans was less fortunate; they struggled to grow food, cope with changing seasons, and live peaceably together.

49

The Troubles of the Fifth Age

In his *Works and Days*, Hesiod vividly described the troubles inherent in his time, the so-called Age of Iron, as well as predicted the inevitable destruction of that fifth and last mythical human period.

Men never rest from labor and sorrow by day, and from perishing by night. And the gods shall lay sore trouble upon them. But, notwithstanding, even these shall have some good mingled with their evils. And Zeus will destroy this race of mortal men also when they come to have grey hair on the temples at their birth. The father will not agree with his children, nor the children with their father, nor guest with his host, nor comrade with comrade. Nor will brother be dear to brother as [in the past]. Men will dishonor their parents as they grow quickly old, and will carp at them, chiding them with bitter words, hard-hearted they, not knowing the fear of the gods. They will not repay their aged parents the cost [of] their nurture, for might shall be their right. And one man will sack another's city. There will be no favor for the man who keeps his oath or for the just or for the good. But rather, men will praise the evil-doer and his violent dealing. Strength will be right and reverence will cease to be.

Hesiod, *Works and Days*, in *Hesiod, The Homeric Hymns, and Homerica,* trans. H.G. Evelyn-White. Cambridge, MA: Harvard University Press, 1964, pp. 15, 17.

These were the structures that the Greeks of that era thought must have been erected by giants. Today it is known that these ruins were the remnants of the palace-citadels of the Bronze Age Minoans and Mycenaeans. When those peoples disappeared, the surviving Greeks fell into poverty and lost both literacy and advanced arts. It was clear to those dark-age Greeks that their own society was inferior to the past one. Likely for that reason they came to firmly believe that civilization's ongoing decay was the natural order of things.

Moreover, the Greeks passed that concept of steady social decline on to later Westerners. As modern mythologist Mark P.O. Morford puts it, thanks to the way the classical Greeks interpreted their mythical past, "this conception of the deterioration of the human race has been potent in subsequent literature, both ancient and modern. The vision of a paradise in a golden age when all was well inevitably holds fascination"[30] for the members of Western societies as a whole.

From Bronze to Iron

In the Five Ages of Men myth, humanity's seemingly inevitable decline continued in the third age, which the classical myth-tellers called the Age of Bronze. (This imaginary era should not be confused with the very real Bronze Age that modern scholars named and described.) In the second age, people had been burdened with daily work and having to deal with cold weather. Now the inhabitants of the third human era, whom Zeus had fashioned from ash trees, were plagued by wars that brought much death and destruction.

In fact, Hesiod wrote, some people actually enjoyed seeing and taking part in "deeds of violence." Many others were "hard of heart like adamant, fearful men. Great was their strength and unconquerable the arms which grew from their shoulders on their strong limbs. Their armor was of bronze, and their houses of bronze, and of bronze were their implements."[31] In time, the story went, Zeus looked at these war-mongering men he had created and had second thoughts. Eventually, he drowned them all in a huge flood.

For a while following that deluge, earth's surface lacked the tread of human feet. Then the fourth period of people began. This was the era the classical Greeks labeled the Age of Heroes because it featured a number of stalwart, bold, and exceedingly brave men. They did their best to right wrongs and better the human condition. It was the world in which a group of Greek kings laid siege to the famous city of Troy, with its towering stone walls; when the fearless strongman Heracles performed his renowned Twelve Labors; and the intrepid Jason and the Argonauts recovered the magical Golden Fleece from a faraway land.

After accomplishing great deeds, most of those heroes departed for the legendary Isles of the Blessed. According to the Greek myths, that paradise-like place was where the gods sent the noblest men following their deaths. There, Hesiod said, they "live untouched by sorrow" near "the shore of deep swirling Ocean, happy heroes for whom the grain-giving earth bears honey-sweet fruit flourishing thrice a year."[32]

An unknown number of years elapsed before the fifth human era, the Age of Iron, began. This was the period in which Hesiod, Homer, and the classical Greeks themselves lived. Hesiod felt it was the worst age of all and that it was bound to end in disaster and desolation. "Bitter sorrows will be left for mortal men, and there will be no help against evil,"[33] he unhappily predicted.

Ongoing Myth Making

In looking at the sequence of the five ages in the myth, it quickly becomes obvious that one of them does not seem to fit. Each is named for a *metallon*, Greek for "metal," except the fourth—the Heroic Age. That period also stands out because its story emphasizes the positive deeds of admirable people—the heroes—rather than wars, corruption, and other negative happenings.

The best-educated classical Greeks were well aware of this inconsistent feature of the Ages of Men tale. They understood that Hesiod's *Works and Days* presented two different kinds of myth intertwined in a single narrative. The first was a very *archaeos*, or ancient, creation tale of four ages of humanity, each named for a metal. The second kind of myth was an original story fabricated by Hesiod himself. Scholar Karen Armstrong explains, "Hesiod created a new version of the [very early Greek] myth of the Four Ages of Men. Traditionally there were four successive eras, each more degenerate than the last. Hesiod altered the story by adding the Heroic Age, which he inserted between the Age of Bronze and the current Age of Iron, the worst era of all."[34]

WORD ORIGINS

metallon

In ancient Greece: the word for metal.

In modern life: metallic, meaning made of metal.

The ancient Greeks saw no reason to doubt that splendid and prosperous kingdoms had once existed in their lands. Myths, and ruins like these, seemed to provide solid evidence of a once-magnificent past.

The classical Greeks, who flourished in the three centuries immediately following Hesiod, accepted his addition of the Heroic Age to the older myth. Like him, they were aware that numerous other myths told of the heroes of the Trojan War, the Argonauts' voyage, the slaying of monsters by various heroes, and so forth. The couple of centuries in which those heroes supposedly lived did not fit into the scheme of the original myth of the four ages. So those centuries had to be added as a fifth age.

This shows clearly that the Greeks recognized that not all creation myths were very ancient. Instead, myth making was an ongoing, fluid process. Another example of this process in their own time was the way Aeschylus and the other great fifth-century-BCE playwrights often mixed new ideas into the old myths they retold in their plays. These additions were intended to make the audiences think about how the themes of the myths related to their social, religious, and political customs. In this way Greek artistic creativity frequently made dusty old stories more relevant to classical Greek thought and opinion.

The Fire Thief

In the second major myth about humanity's creation, the Titan Prometheus was the central character. According to the story, Zeus recognized that the older god possessed unusual wisdom and for that reason made him his chief advisor. The leader of the Olympians also viewed Prometheus as the right individual to carry out an important

Myth-Tellers' Corner: Aeschylus

Aeschylus, who was born in about 525 BCE, earned a reputation in his own day as the world's first great playwright, an opinion that modern experts still hold. As a young man, he fought in the famous battle of Marathon, in 490 BCE. There a small Athenian army crushed a larger force of invading Persians. The playwright also took part in the huge naval battle at Salamis (near Athens) ten years later, an event he described later in the *Persians* (472 BCE). In addition to that work, only six of his other reputed total of more than eighty plays survive today. The six are *Agamemnon* (458 BCE), the *Libation Bearers* (458 BCE), the *Eumenides* (458 BCE), *Seven Against Thebes* (467 BCE), *The Suppliant Women* (circa 463 BCE), and *Prometheus Bound* (circa 460 BCE). All of these works relied heavily on the old Greek myths, and *Prometheus Bound* retold, as well as added to, the major creation myth involving the Titan Prometheus. Aeschylus also introduced a number of theatrical ideas. Before him, a single actor portrayed all of a play's major roles by wearing different masks. His innovation was to use a second actor, who also wore several masks. That allowed a playwright to show more characters, in the process making the story more complex.

task—fashioning a race of mortal beings. Prometheus was glad to take the job and proceeded to construct the first human bodies from mud. Then he hurried away into the sky, planning to keep an eye on his new creations and see how they fared in building a civilization.

At first Prometheus was optimistic that the humans would do well and be happy. But the longer he watched them, the sadder he became because they underwent a constant struggle simply to stay alive. They almost froze to death in wintertime and frequently had to defend themselves against attacks by bears, lions, and other wild animals. Metal weapons would have helped, the god realized, not only for defense but also to hunt small creatures to eat. But the humans had neither metal weapons nor *organa*, or tools, because they knew nothing about fire, which was needed to melt down and shape the metals.

Prometheus wanted to introduce fire to his beloved creations. But Zeus forbade it, saying that only the immortal gods should have access to that powerful natural force. At first the Titan followed his boss's order. But eventually, Prometheus could stand it no more. He boldly snuck behind Zeus's back, took some fire from a hearth on Mount Olympus, and gave it to the humans. The creator god also taught them how to erect hearths of their own, how to cook their food, and how to make tools and weapons. As a result, the humans were able to build a bustling civilization.

When Zeus found out what had happened, he was furious. He ordered that Prometheus be chained to an enormous rock on a faraway mountain. Thereafter, each day a large vulture (or in some ancient sources an eagle) tore out the captive's liver. That vital organ grew back each night, only to be torn out again the next day.

> ## WORD ORIGINS
>
> ### archaeos
>
> In ancient Greece: the term for ancient.
>
> In modern life: archaic, meaning very old; and archaeology, the study of past ages.

Making Moral Choices

During Athens's great cultural outburst in the fifth century BCE, this moving myth of Prometheus's courage and sacrifice became the subject of one of the greatest plays ever written. Titled *Prometheus Bound*, it was written by the master dramatist Aeschylus. He emphasized the title character's love and pity for his human creations and his great courage in standing up to Zeus. In the play, Zeus offers to liberate the chained god from the cliff if he will do the lord of Olympus various favors. But Prometheus refuses as a matter of principle. Giving fire to people was the morally right thing to do, he insists.

Prometheus defied Zeus when he gave fire to human beings. As punishment, he was chained to a rock and forced to endure his liver being torn out by a vulture and growing back again over and over until the end of time.

Watching this powerful drama unfold, many Greek playgoers felt a connection to Prometheus, seeing his struggle against injustice as similar in some ways to their own life experiences. They agreed that doing the right thing, no matter what the consequences, was ideally best. Also, they hoped that, faced with a hard choice, they might display the kind of courage that Prometheus did.

This impulse to do the right, ethical thing whenever possible—a notable character trait of many classical Greeks—did not stem from their religious convictions. Indeed, the Greeks were not impelled to make difficult moral choices in hopes of gaining a ticket to a happy afterlife. Rather, they were taught from childhood that acting honorably should be a reward in and of itself. Displaying a lack of honor was a social taboo because it reflected badly on one's family reputation. Thus, Prometheus's creation story, along with various other Greek myths, provided people with moral examples in the same way that some biblical tales do for Jews and Christians.

WORD ORIGINS

Prometheus

In ancient Greece: the clever Titan who created humans from mud and showed them how to use fire.

In modern life: promethean, meaning a clever, innovative person.

Chapter Five

Survival of the Greek Myths

The ancient Greek creation myths, along with other mythical tales the Greeks had collected over many centuries, survived the on-rushing tide of later ages, peoples, religions, and cultures, and they remain popular today. The reasons for this remarkable survival are many and complex. But overall the process by which it happened can be summarized in two general stages.

In the first stage, the creation myths lost their relevance and power as widely accepted accounts of how the cosmos, gods, and humans arose. That is, people came to see them merely as folktales and looked elsewhere for explanations of how the world and people originated. In the second stage of the Greek myths' evolution, which overlapped with the first, these stories perpetually passed from one generation to another. This occurred in large part because people still found them entertaining. Also, scholars of history, literature, and religion continued to study those ancient tales in an effort to understand the development of past cultures.

As a result of these trends, the Greek creation myths came to be translated into nearly every language. Also, especially in Europe and the places around the globe colonized by Europeans (generally referred to as Western civilization), those stories were taught in schools and retold in poems, novels, plays, and music. In the twentieth century, moreover, the same myths became fodder for movies, television shows, comic books, video games, and other forms of entertainment. In short, they have become part of the very fabric of modern Western culture.

The Myths Mere Fables?

The first stage in the Greek creation myths' survival began in a quiet, unassuming way in the sixth century BCE. During those years, early Greek scientists like Thales and Anaximander started to question traditional views of the cosmos. These included its structure, its chief elements, and how it had come to be.

Regarding that latter point, these early rational thinkers suspected that the world, people, and *zoia*, or animals, were created by natural forces of some kind. So the age-old explanations presented in the creation myths might well be little more than fables. As one noted modern scholar summarizes it, "The great contribution of the sixth-century BCE Greek thinkers [was] their determination to abandon the mythological and religious framework and attempt instead to explain the world by material processes alone. [They] sought to enthrone human reason as the tool for understanding the universe and to replace divine plan with material forces."[35]

In the centuries that followed, Greek science cast more and more doubt on the reality of the traditional creation stories. This trend was reinforced by the rise of literary scholarship in Greece and in Rome, which absorbed the Greek city-states and kingdoms in the second and first centuries BCE. Philosophers and writers did retell and/or mention the old myths. But these intellectuals were fully convinced that the events and characters in those tales had never been factual or real. Like modern scholars, they were primarily interested in explaining how the myths had originated and affected religion and society.

Particularly influential among these ancient thinkers was a Greek named Euhemerus, who lived in the late fourth century BCE. He

WORD ORIGINS

zoia

In ancient Greece: the word for animals.

In modern life: zoo, meaning a place where animals are on public display; and *zoology*, the scientific study of animals.

proposed that the traditional gods in the creation tales were actually once people—kings, queens, military heroes, and so forth. They had been inflated into deities, he said, over long years of exaggeration in repeated retellings of their deeds. Euhemerus's ideas and writings were quite popular for several centuries, which struck a major blow to the historical credibility of the traditional creation myths.

"True" Tales Versus "False" Ones

Even more damaging to the Greek creation stories was the rise of Christianity, which became the principal faith of the Roman Empire in the late fourth century CE. In the final years of that century, Christian emperors prohibited people from openly worshipping the Greco-Roman gods. A great many of the realm's residents—Greeks and Romans alike—continued to revere those deities in private. But by this time, they no longer accepted the traditional creation myths as having actually happened.

Fortunately for later ages, however, both non-Christians, or pagans, and some Christian churchmen continued to retell those old stories and hand them down to later generations. The pagans did so because they felt the myths were a crucial aspect of their cultural heritage. Meanwhile, Christian thinkers, writers, and monks had their own uses for the ancient myths. One approach was to place the old Greek tale of Chaos, Eros, Gaea, and Uranus side by side with the creation story in Genesis, the Bible's first book. That comparison supposedly showed how the "true" biblical tale was superior to the "false" pagan one.

Later still, following Rome's fall in the fifth and sixth centuries, medieval monks and other churchmen used the Greek creation myths for a different purpose. The characters and events from those tales became tools intended give a clergyman's own writings and lectures

WORD ORIGINS

Euhemerus

In ancient Greece: a philosopher who proposed that the mythical Greek gods were human rulers and heroes whose reputations were exaggerated over time.

In modern life: euhemerism, a belief that mythical characters are based on historical ones; and euhemerist, someone who accepts that idea.

Myth-Tellers' Corner: Euhemerus

The Greek thinker and writer Euhemerus lived from about 330 to 260 BCE. His major work, the *Sacred History,* in which he retold and discussed various creation tales and other myths, is lost. But fragments of his distinctive theory about the myths survive in the work of the first-century-BCE Greek historian Diodorus Siculus. According to Diodorus, many Greek scholars thought the gods were "eternal and imperishable, such as the sun and moon and the other stars of the heavens." Moreover, because those deities were immortal, they endured "from everlasting to everlasting." In contrast, Diodorus explained, Euhemerus believed that the gods mentioned in the creation myths—Eros, Gaea, Uranus, and so forth—were

> terrestrial beings who attained to immortal honor and fame because of their benefactions [positive gifts] to mankind. . . . Euhemerus goes on to say that Uranus was the first to be king, that he was an honorable man and beneficent [helpful and just], who was versed in the movement of the stars, and that he was also the first to honor the gods of the heavens with sacrifices, whence he was called Uranus or "Heaven." There were born to him by his wife Hestia two sons, Titan and Cronos, and two daughters, Rhea and Demeter. Cronos became king after Uranus, and marrying Rhea he begat Zeus and Hera and Poseidon.

Diodorus Siculus, *Library of History,* trans. C.H. Oldfather, Theoi Greek Mythology. www.theoi.com.

a learned air. Indeed, the ability to quote from an ancient Greco-Roman story was now a sign of an educated, cultured individual.

Painters and the Mythical Creation

It was during the last stage of the medieval era—the Renaissance (circa 1300–1600)—that European society began openly and eagerly to utilize the characters and events of the Greek creation myths. That period witnessed a large-scale flowering of literature and the fine arts. Writers, painters, sculptors, and other creative individuals came to employ Greek mythical themes and references in their works. This further popularized those old stories and promoted both teaching them in schools and learning about them by word of mouth outside of formal education.

Of the various kinds of Renaissance artists, painters were particularly enthusiastic about portraying characters from the Greek creation tales. One of the best known of those talented individuals was a fifteenth-century Italian, Sandro Botticelli. At some point between 1482 and 1486, he completed a large (7 by 10 feet, or 2 by 3 m) work titled *Spring*. It shows an imaginary gathering of nine mythical Greek deities in a lush, wooded garden fashioned shortly after earth's creation.

Botticelli became even more famous for his magnificent painting *The Birth of Venus*. Like many artists of his era, he used the Roman names for the Greek gods, in this case substituting the Roman Venus for Aphrodite, the Greek name for the goddess of love and beauty. In the original Greek creation story about the rise of the Titans, after Cronos castrated his father, Uranus, the wounded sky god's severed parts fell into the sea. Soon afterward, a mass of foam bubbled up from that spot. Then out of the foam stepped Aphrodite, shown in the painting standing naked atop a large clamshell.

A later major Renaissance painter, Italy's Giorgio Vasari, tackled a different moment from the same creation myth. His 1560 work *The Mutilation of Uranus* depicts Cronos swinging a sickle at his father as a bevy of other Titans looks on. For reasons that are uncertain, Cronos and other Titans were unusually favored subjects of painters both during and after the Renaissance. German artist Peter Paul Rubens's 1638 work *Cronos Devouring One of His Children* is a popular example. American painter John Singer Sargent's *Atlas and the Hesperides* (1925) is another.

Some painters even portrayed the ancient Greek myth makers, including Homer, Hesiod, and Aeschylus and the other great fifth-century-BCE Athenian playwrights. Particularly popular and memorable among these works is *Hesiod and the Muses* (1860), by noted French artist Gustave Moreau. The painting shows the renowned farmer-poet meeting with the

Renaissance artists such as Sandro Botticelli portrayed many characters from Greek creation stories in their art. Botticelli's painting, The Birth of Venus, *depicts the emergence into the world of Aphrodite (known to the Romans as Venus), the goddess of love and beauty.*

female deities he claimed inspired him to write about the creation of the world and gods.

Literary Allusions to the Myths

During the past four to five centuries, the period that most historians call modern times, painting has been only one of the numerous artistic media employed to retell or depict the ancient Greek creation stories. Others have included sculpture, poetry, short stories, novels, stage plays, musical pieces, radio dramas, television shows, movies, comic books, graphic novels, and video games. In some cases an entire poem, novel, play, or movie has told part or all of a creation myth. In many other cases characters or events from those tales have appeared in brief allusions—specific references to or quotations from the myths.

Such allusions have been especially plentiful in various forms of literature. For instance, notable examples appear throughout the plays of one of the great literary masters—English playwright William Shakespeare. One of the more striking examples comes from his 1603 play *Othello*, in which the title character marries a woman named Desdemona. As the tangled plot unfolds, he mistakenly thinks she has cheated on him; and in the end he kills her for it. Just before committing that awful deed, he watches her sleep and says, "Once put out thy light, thou cunning pattern of excelling nature, I know not where is that Promethean heat that can thy light relume [reilluminate]."[36]

The English playwright William Shakespeare makes allusions to Prometheus, the god credited with shaping humans from mud, in Othello. *Here, in a scene from the play, Othello speaks with his beloved Desdemona.*

Here the author alludes to Prometheus, the god credited with shaping humans from mud. By "Promethean heat," Shakespeare means the spark of life within his wife. According to scholars Barbara A. Mowat and Paul Werstine, "Shakespeare seems to be combining two specific myths about Prometheus, one in which Prometheus gave fire to humankind and one in which he was the creator of humankind."[37]

Shakespeare alluded to Prometheus numerous other times in his plays. Indeed, he referenced a single Promethean incident—the vulture tearing out the chained god's liver—no less than five times in various plays. One of these allusions is from the comedy *The Merry Wives of Windsor*, in which one character angrily tells another, "Let vultures grip thy guts!"[38] Another example comes from the tragedy *Titus Andronicus*, in which a character tortured by doubt refers to "the gnawing vulture of my mind."[39]

The Creator Deity in Popular Culture

It turns out that references to Prometheus by Shakespeare and other writers constitute only the tip of the proverbial iceberg of the appearances of that god within Western culture. The colorful Titan is only one of dozens of characters in the Greek creation myths, of course. Yet he has long been and remains one of the more popular of their number. Moreover, tracing just a few of the thousands of allusions to him in modern culture demonstrates the incredible degree to which those tales have become imbedded in Western civilization's framework.

Indeed, paintings alone of Prometheus and his exploits number at least in the hundreds. One of the more noted examples is Rubens's 1611 work showing the vulture attacking the chained deity. Luca Giordano's 1666 painting and Moreau's 1867 masterpiece depict that same gruesome scene from different angles. Prometheus steals the Olympian fire in Jan Cossiers's renowned 1636 canvas, while Louis de Silvestre's 1701 painting, now held by the Getty Museum in Los Angeles, shows the Titan creating humans.

Of the many sculptures based on Prometheus's creation myths, probably the most recognizable to most people is the one that dominates the Lower Plaza of Rockefeller Center in New York City. It was fashioned in 1934 by the late noted American sculptor Paul Manship. Weighing a whopping 8 tons (7.3 metric tons), the stunning gilded bronze work depicts the god clutching heavenly fire on his way to present it to humanity.

Filmmakers and video gamers have also been fascinated by the Prometheus myths. The most recent major filmic example is popular movie director Ridley Scott's 2012 film, *Prometheus*. The big-budget movie utilizes the theme of the mythical Titan giving life—what Greeks called *bios*—to humans. In the film, *Prometheus*, a spaceship from earth's future, investigates an alien race trying to create human life, a clear parallel to the myth.

WORD ORIGINS

bios

In ancient Greece: the word for life.

In modern life: biology, the study of living things.

Another of Prometheus's famous mythical experiences is explored in the 2007 video game *God of War II*, developed by Santa Monica Studios in California. The hero of the story that unfolds in the game—Kratos—comes upon Prometheus, who is chained to a huge rock. The Titan explains that his insides are consumed each day by a vulture, a fate inflicted by Zeus to punish Prometheus for giving fire to humans. Kratos then helps to free the tortured Titan. (By contrast, in mythology the strongman Heracles frees Prometheus.)

Modern artists, filmmakers, and video game makers have not been alone in their use of the Promethean creation myths. Scientists have also exploited the Titan's connection to the divine force of fire in the age-old story. In the years following radioactivity's discovery in the late 1800s, many people saw a parallel between that newly discovered phenomenon and fire, as Zeus, Prometheus, and the early gods viewed it. Both natural forces seemed to possess almost mystical properties. Not surprisingly, therefore, scientists named the radioactive element confirmed by English physicist Harry Moseley in 1914 promethium, after the mythical creator deity.

Similarly, some scientists and other modern individuals with reputations for amassing unusually large amounts of knowledge tapped into that same god's mythical reputation for wisdom and forethought. In 1982 American philosopher Ronald K. Hoeflin established the Prometheus Society. Its members are people who have managed to score extremely high on IQ tests, written examinations designed to

Prometheus in Outer Space

Director Ridley Scott's 2012 film *Prometheus* exploited that ancient god's creation myths in important ways, says writer and filmmaker Govindini Murty, who also mentions various well-known literary works based on those tales. In the movie, Murty explains,

> as the spaceship Prometheus approaches the moon LV-223, Peter Weyland, the wealthy businessman funding the venture, addresses the crew in a video. He explains the myth of Prometheus, and says to them mysteriously, "the time has now come for his return." In ancient Greek myth Prometheus was a Titan who … defied the gods by stealing fire from Olympus and giving it to humanity. Aeschylus' play *Prometheus Bound* depicts Prometheus as a mad rebel against divine authority.

This fairly critical portrayal of Prometheus is later reversed in nineteenth-century writer Percy Shelley's poem *Prometheus Unbound*, which presents Prometheus as a compassionate character and defender of humans. Murty continues,

> There are multiple Prometheus figures in the movie, from the mysterious race of engineers who appear to have been struck down after using a lethal bio-technology, to Elizabeth Shaw who defies the limits of science to acquire potentially dangerous information about human origins, to Peter Weyland who wishes to gain forbidden knowledge of immortality to make himself equivalent to the gods. Finally, a scene in which Shaw and her fellow scientists attempt to animate the head of one of the engineers with electricity appears drawn from Mary Shelley's *Frankenstein*—subtitled, "The Modern Prometheus."

Govindini Murty, "Decoding the Cultural Influences in *Prometheus*, from Lovecraft to *Halo*," *Atlantic*, June 11, 2012. www.theatlantic.com.

The spaceship Prometheus *in the 2012 movie of the same name offers a striking example of the enduring role of Greek mythology in popular culture. The film revolves around an alien race that is trying to create human life.*

measure intelligence. Fittingly, the organization's official publication, published ten times per year, is called the *Gift of Fire*.

Products of Ancient Imagination

By no means is Prometheus the only character from the Greek creation myths who has been widely exploited in medieval and modern culture. Literary, artistic, and other allusions to Gaea, Cronos, Atlas, Zeus, Poseidon, Athena, and several others abound as well. Most of these references are as plentiful, or nearly so, as those involving the Titan who was said to have fashioned humanity.

In fact, these abundant references to the Greek creation myths, when combined with allusions to other surviving Greek myths, make up a substantial portion of the arts, literature, and other creative aspects of Western civilization. "Even the briefest survey" of the modern uses of those ancient tales Mark P.O. Morford points out, "cannot help but forcefully remind us [of] the potent inspiration that mythology provides for all facets of creative artistic expression."[40]

The late prolific historian Michael Grant agreed. He added that Western culture would simply not be what it is today without the countless shards of ancient Greek myth deeply imbedded within it. "Without these myths," he explained, "we would be hard put to understand the arts and literature and ways of thinking of the West" during the many centuries that elapsed "since the Classical world came to an end." Over and over again, Grant concluded, "these products of ancient imagination have been used to inspire fresh creative efforts, which amount to a substantial part of our whole cultural inheritance."[41]

Source Notes

Introduction: Origins of the Creation Tales

1. Hesiod, *Theogony*, in *Hesiod and Theognis*, trans. Dorothea Wender. New York: Penguin, 1982, p. 26.

Chapter One: The Cosmos and Earth Emerge

2. Rhoda A. Hendricks, ed. and trans., *Classical Gods and Heroes: Myths as Told by the Ancient Authors*. New York: Morrow Quill, 1974, p. 11.

3. Michael Grant and John Hazel, *Who's Who in Classical Mythology*. London: Weidenfeld and Nicolson, 1973, p. 7.

4. Grant and Hazel, *Who's Who in Classical Mythology*, pp. 7–8.

5. Edith Hamilton, *Mythology*. New York: Grand Central, 1999, p. 24.

6. W.H.D. Rouse, *Gods, Heroes and Men of Ancient Greece*. New York: New American Library, 2001, p. 11.

7. Aristophanes, *Birds*, lines 693–95, trans. Don Nardo.

8. Aristophanes, *Birds*, lines 698–702.

9. Plato, *Timaeus*, in *The Dialogues of Plato*, trans. Benjamin Jowett. Chicago: Encyclopedia Britannica, 1952, p. 447.

10. Plato, *Timaeus*, p. 447.

11. Plato, *Timaeus*, p. 447.

12. Hesiod, *Theogony*, trans. Wender, p. 27.

13. Quoted in Theoi Greek Mythology, "Gaia Earth & Cult." www.theoi.com.

14. Hesiod, *Theogony*, trans. Wender, p. 27.

Chapter Two: The Rise of the Titans

15. Homer, *Iliad*, Book 21, lines 194–95, trans. Don Nardo.

16. Quoted in Theoi Greek Mythology, "Atlas." www.theoi.com.

17. Hesiod, *Theogony*, in *Hesiod, The Homeric Hymns, and Homerica*, trans. H.G. Evelyn-White. Cambridge, MA: Harvard University Press, 1964, pp. 91, 93.

18. Pausanias, *Guide to Greece*, vol. 1, trans. Peter Levi. New York: Penguin, 1971, p. 446.

Chapter Three: The Olympians Take Charge

19. Homer, *Iliad*, Book 5, lines 440–42.

20. Quoted in Theoi Greek Mythology, "Callimachus Hymns 1–3." www.theoi.com.

21. Hesiod, *Theogony*, trans. Wender, p. 39.

22. Hesiod, *Theogony*, trans. Evelyn-White, p. 47.

23. Aeschylus, *Prometheus Bound*, in *Aeschylus: Prometheus Bound, The Suppliants, Seven Against Thebes, The Persians*, trans. Philip Vellacott. Baltimore: Penguin, 1961, p. 27.

24. Aeschylus, *Prometheus Bound*, p. 27.

25. Hesiod, *Theogony*, trans. Evelyn-White, pp. 129, 131.

26. Hesiod, *Theogony*, trans. Evelyn-White, p. 131.

27. Hesiod, *Theogony*, trans. Wender, pp. 46–47.

Chapter Four: Crafting the Human Race

28. Hesiod, *Works and Days*, in *Hesiod, The Homeric Hymns, and Homerica*, trans. H.G. Evelyn-White. Cambridge, MA: Harvard University Press, 1964, p. 11.

29. Hesiod, *Works and Days*, p. 13.

30. Mark P.O. Morford and Robert J. Lenardon, *Classical Mythology*. New York: Oxford University Press, 2010, p. 43.

31. Hesiod, *Works and Days*, p. 13.

32. Hesiod, *Works and Days*, p. 15.

33. Hesiod, *Works and Days*, p. 17.

34. Karen Armstrong, *The Great Transformation: The Beginning of Our Religious Traditions*. New York: Doubleday, 2006, p. 141.

Chapter Five: Survival of the Greek Myths

35. Sarah B. Pomeroy et al., *Ancient Greece: A Political, Social, and Cultural History*. New York: Oxford University Press, 2007, p. 258.

36. William Shakespeare, *Othello*, Act 5, scene 2, lines 10–13.

37. Barbara A. Mowat and Paul Werstine, eds., *Othello by William Shakespeare*. New York: Simon and Schuster, 2011, p. 236.

38. William Shakespeare, *The Merry Wives of Windsor*, Act 1, scene 3, line 42.

39. William Shakespeare, *Titus Andronicus*, Act 5, scene 2, line 31.

40. Morford and Lenardon, *Classical Mythology*, p. 491.

41. Michael Grant, *Myths of the Greeks and Romans*. New York: Plume, 1995, p. xvii.

For Further Research

Books

Arthur Cotterell, *The Illustrated A–Z of Classic Mythology*. Leicester, UK: Lorenz, 2014.

Kathleen N. Daly, *Greek and Roman Mythology A to Z*. New York: Chelsea House, 2009.

Delphi Classics, *Delphi Complete Works of Hesiod*. East Sussex, UK: Delphi Classics, 2013.

Edith Hamilton, *Mythology*. New York: Grand Central, 2011.

Sarah Maguire, *In the Beginning Was Chaos: Greek Myths of the Gods and Creation*. New York: Amazon Digital Services, 2015.

Mark P.O. Morford and Robert J. Lenardon, *Classical Mythology*. New York: Oxford University Press, 2010.

Donna Jo Napoli, *Treasury of Greek Mythology: Classic Stories of Gods, Goddesses, Heroes, and Monsters*. New York: National Geographic, 2011.

Kathleen Sears, *Mythology 101: From Gods and Goddesses to Monsters and Mortals, Your Guide to Ancient Mythology*. Fort Collins, CO: Adams Media, 2014.

Marcia Williams, *Greek Myths*. Somerville, MA: Candlewick, 2011.

Internet Sources

Ancient Origins, "Greek Mythology and Human Origins." www.ancient-origins.net/human-origins-folklore/greek-mythology-and-human-origins-0064.

Bamber Gascoigne, "Creation Stories," Historyworld. www.historyworld.net/wrldhis/PlainTextHistories.asp?ParagraphID=bjh.

Theoi Greek Mythology, "Major Titans." www.theoi.com/greek-my
thology/titans.html.

Websites

Greek Mythology Link (www.maicar.com/GML/index.html). This
well-thought-out site has a biographical dictionary with more than
six thousand entries and some forty-five hundred photos, drawings,
and other images.

Medea's Lair: Tales of Greek Mythology (www.medeaslair.net
/myths.html). The authors of this site do a nice job of retelling the old
myths, which are grouped into categories that include "Men and Heroes," "Tales of Love and Loss," and "Giants and Beasts."

Mythweb Encyclopedia of Greek Mythology (www.mythweb.com
/encyc). This website provides a lot of useful information about both
major and minor Greek mythological characters.

Theoi Greek Mythology (www.theoi.com). This is the most comprehensive and reliable general website about Greek mythology on the
Internet. It features hundreds of separate pages filled with detailed,
accurate information, as well as numerous primary sources.

Index

Picture Credits

Cover: akg-images/Rabatti-Domingie/Newscom

6: Maury Aaseng

9: The Fall of the Giants (La caduta dei giganti), by Guido Reni, 1636–1637, 17th Century, oil on canvas, 204 x 182 cm/Mondadori Portfolio/Bridgeman Images

15: The Chaos, engraved by Bernard Picart (1673–1733), 1731 (engraving), Diepenbeeck, Abraham Jansz van. (1596–1675)/Private Collection/The Stapleton Collection/Bridgeman Images

19: © Pascal Deloche/Godong/Corbis

23: Apollo slaying Python, Payne, Roger (b.1934)/Private Collection/© Look and Learn/Bridgeman Images

27: © Marc Dozier/Hemis/Corbis

31: © Historical Picture Archive/Corbis

34: © Corbis

38: Depositphotos

41: The figure of the goddess was a colossal one, illustration from 'The Story of Greece' by Mary Macgregor, 1st edition, 1913 (colour print), Crane, Walter (1845–1915)/Private Collection/The Stapleton Collection/Bridgeman Images

44: © GraphicaArts/Corbis

49: © Stephano Bianchetti/Corbis

53: Shutterstock/Havoc

56: Prometheus carrying fire (oil), Cossiers, Jan (1600–71)/Prado, Madrid, Spain/Index/Bridgeman Images

63: © The Gallery Collection/Corbis

64: © Christie's Images/Corbis

68: Photofest Images

About the Author

Classical historian Don Nardo has written numerous acclaimed volumes about ancient civilizations and peoples. They include more than a dozen overviews of the mythologies of the Sumerians, Babylonians, Egyptians, Greeks, Romans, Persians, and others. Nardo also composes and arranges orchestral music. He lives with his wife, Christine, in Massachusetts.